CONTENTS

DEDICATION

For Steve Sardell, being my first real good friend when I moved to the Low Country, always offering a wealth of knowledge and insight.

For Bob Delmar, I always looked up to him as the older brother I never had, who was always eager to discuss history.

For "Low Country Joe" Yocius, a great mentor and friend who as helped me in countless situations.

For Michael McChesney, giving twenty years of service for the United States and partaking in the same interests that I enjoy.

ACKNOWLEDGMENTS

I would like to thank Caroline Warner for giving me some information on her ancestral roots in the Low Country. The Library of Congress' online catalog provided a great many photographs, many I have never seen published before. Thanks and gratitude goes out for Joe Yocius, Low Country Joe, for opening up Daufuskie Island and always allowing me to explore the sites. Gratitude goes out for Tom Paxton, allowing Ben as a passenger, in his helicopter to take photographs at 110 mph, allowing us to offer a different perspective of where these events occurred. Thanks goes out to Christie Brown of the Heyward House Historic Center in Bluffton by opening up the archives for some of the family histories of the families that lived here when war came to the Low Country. I would also like to thank Mary Ann Solem and Jeff Thomas for allowing us to photograph the Cuthbert House Bed and Breakfast in Beaufort. Many thanks go out to the staff at the Georgia Historical Society and to the staff of the Chatham County Library on Bull Street. Thanks go out to David Kemmerley, a fellow Civil War historian, who was great to bounce ideas off of.

PREFACE

The concept of this book grew out of the research for *Civil War Walking Tour of Savannah*. We ran across some of the same people from the Civil War period that influenced both Savannah and the South Carolina Low Country. A great number of the area residential communities were named after former plantations that existed before the war. Ben had an extraordinary experience; he was able to fly in a helicopter at 110 miles per hour photographing sites from an aerial perspective. It was very interesting to explore some of the properties that people had owned before the war, and to know that four years later, these same people had virtually nothing. Former slaves and carpetbaggers alike paid the back taxes to obtain these grand homes. A good many of these homes survive, leaving a vision of a time that has passed into the ages.

Personally, I was able to explore ground that was once traversed by an ancestor of mine; for three months in early 1863 he served with the 81st New York Infantry at Fort Mitchell on Hilton Head Island. He later fought with the Army of the James until the end of the war.

Many military actions occurred here, such as the landings on Hilton Head. It was the largest amphibious operation undertaken by the United States until the June 6, 1944, Normandy landings.

Union forces, if they had the support, could easily have cut off either Charleston or Savannah from their bases in the Low Country. This never happened because the supplies and troops were assigned to the armies fighting in Virginia and Tennessee in 1862, a missed opportunity.

There were many discoveries on my part. This fact finding allowed me to appreciate even more the atmosphere of the South Carolina Low Country in both war and peace.

INTRODUCTION

Early in the eighteenth century, many settlers came into the Low Country to find their fortune by planting rice. By the time of the Revolutionary War, South Carolina was Great Britain's most profitable colony. Rice would continue to support the Southern plantation system and would only be surpassed after the cotton gin was invented in Savannah. Through the first part of the nineteenth century, cotton and rice were the United States' greatest exports. The slaves that first arrived in the Low Country had originated from the West Indies, Cuba, and West Africa.[1]

These plantation families controlled these lands until Federal forces arrived in November 1861. Some of the plantation homes were torched by the retreating Confederate defenders.[2] Today many of the residential communities, beaches, and parks in the Low Country are named after former plantations. Union troops assigned here enjoyed crab boils, shrimp, and red fish.

The rice commodity became the early staple of South Carolina economics. The rice plantations were located on fresh water rivers and creeks that were tidal. Dikes and dams were constructed to bring water twice a day to the rice fields. These rice plantations ceased to exist after the war; only traces of the dikes still exist.

Cotton plantations swelled throughout the Deep South after planters realized how much profit they could turn. These planters involved in the growing of cotton became extremely wealthy. In 1860, Hilton Head Island had over twenty, and Daufuskie Island had eleven, plantations that grew the long-staple cotton, also known as Sea Island cotton. The seed had been imported from the island of Anguilla by planters in both South Carolina and Georgia; it carried a higher price and was more desirable.[3]

Many of the smaller plantations had been absorbed by fifteen larger families on Hilton Head, which was one of the most productive areas growing Sea Island cotton. Few of the owners had permanent homes.[4] Planters allowed Palmetto trees to stand, providing shade for the infants as the women worked the fields. Today only ruins dot the Low Country landscape.

Bluffton's "Secession" tree, some of the first dialogue on leaving the Union occurred here.

Right:
A slave-made dike used to transport fresh water to rice plantations on the New River.

Battles flags of two nations at war in the South Carolina Low Country.

Dikes were controlled by high tides when moving water to the rice fields.

Slaves prepare cotton for the gin. *Courtesy of the Library of Congress*.

Cotton was the South's primary cash crop in 1860.

Chapter 1

THE BURNING OF BLUFFTON WALKING TOUR

"For fifty years Bluffton has been spoiling for a fight. And now I think she has got it. That is the center spot of the fire-eaters, Barnwell Rhett's and all that."[5]

**Old Mr. Chestnut on the
Federal landings on Hilton Head**

From I-95 or SC 170, exit onto US 278 East towards Hilton Head Island, follow 278 until it intersects with SC 46. Turn right onto SC 46 West; travel 1.7 miles to the four way stop sign at the traffic circle. Continue straight ahead for another .4 miles; you are now on Boundary Street. Make a right onto Bridge Street and make the next left onto Calhoun Street, park near the church on your right. Walk towards the river.

As you head east on 278 you will pass Rose Hill Plantation on your left; it was known as "Kirk's Folly" before the war. Dr. John Kirk owned it; he anticipated opening the property as a hunting lodge, but it was not completed until the war was over. Local legend suggests that it escaped burning because the Yankees instructed to burn it found it too beautiful to destroy.

The town of Bluffton was established before the war as a community for plantations owners who escaped the summer heat and the threat of fever. They chose this location because of its access to the May River. Summer breezes off the river cooled theses magnificent homes. The town was incorporated in 1852; originally it was known as "Kirk's Bluff."[6]

After the fall of Hilton Head, small raiding parties of Confederates rowed across Skull Creek from Bluffton at night, setting fires to the crops and houses that they had left behind. The raids later became more numerous throughout the coastal islands along the Atlantic. They wanted to deprive the Union government from selling the cotton and using it to fund their war effort. Beaufort native, Stephen Elliot, was credited with burning nineteen plantation homes in one night after leading a raid from Bluffton.[7]

STOP 1:

THE MAY RIVER

"Bluffton in ruins—the destruction of property on Bull's Island some days ago and the recent raid on the Combahee, involving an immense loss of property, is followed by the burning of the beautiful town of Bluffton on May River. This latest outrage took place on Thursday morning last, and resulted in the loss of about forty private residences and nearly one hundred outhouses, stores, etc. We have succeeded in obtaining a list of the property owners who have suffered by the burning of their beautiful houses and settlement." **R. B. Rhett in the *Charleston Mercury*, June 6, 1863.**[8]

From the May River head over to the church nearby.

The town was almost destroyed by federal gunboats on the May River in 1863.[9] The Yankees' five gunboats covered the landing of three companies of infantry on June 3; the force was part of a much larger force that had landed on Hunting Island, near Beaufort.

The May River was used as a highway for Union raiding parties in Bluffton.

13

The force was observed by pickets of the 3rd and 4th South Carolina Cavalry. They moved to engage the threat, but failed to arrive in time to protect Bluffton. A small force of the 11th South Carolina Infantry did exchange shots with the landing party, but the town was largely unprotected and homes were quickly set fire along the river.[10] Union troops had fired forty homes in the Bluffton area.

STOP 2:

THE CHURCH OF THE CROSS, 110 CALHOUN STREET

This church was built in 1857. The church was protected from Union troops trying to set fires in June 1863.[11] Local residents claimed that a heavy growth of trees nearby protected the church from a fire that was set by the raiders.

From the church turn left on to Water Street and stop at the first house on your left.

The Church of the Cross was built in 1857.
Nearby trees helped prevent the burning of the church on June 3, 1863.

STOP 3:
THE HUGER HOUSE,
9 WATER STREET

This home was built in 1855 and was owned during the war by Colonel E. M. Seabrook. This house was the only antebellum house located on the bluff to survive the burning of Bluffton by Federal forces on June 3, 1863. There are Minnie balls lodged in the studs near the front door, an indication that rifle fire was exchanged by Confederate pickets and the Union forces. The house was sold to Doctor Joseph A. Huger in 1882.

The Huger House was built in 1855. Minnie balls are lodged in the studs from the raid of June 3, 1863.

Turn around on Water Street and stop at the house on the corner of Water and Calhoun Streets, the last house on the left before turning left onto Calhoun Street.

STOP 4:

THE ALLEN-LOCKWOOD HOUSE, 94 CALHOUN STREET

This summer home was built in 1850 by William Gaston Allen and his wife, Susan Virginia Bolan. Colonel Allen was a successful planter of the May River Neck area. They previously owned a 300-acre plantation called Garvey Hall. After the war, the couple was bankrupt and was forced to sell their home in 1873.

This summer home was built in 1850; it took advantage of the breeze off the May River.

Continue to walk up Calhoun Street, stopping at the house on the corner of Calhoun and Allen Streets.

STOP 5:
SEVEN OAKS,
82 CALHOUN STREET

This home was built in 1860 for Colonel Middleton Stuart and his wife, the former Emma Barnwell Stoney. She had inherited her father's plantation, Otterburn.

They never returned after the war. They escaped Bluffton after the fall of Hilton Head.

Seven Oaks was built in 1860. Its occupants escaped after the fall of Hilton Head.

Ladies enjoying a walk in Bluffton before war came in November 1861.

Continue up Calhoun Street, crossing Bridge and Green Streets. Turn left onto Lawrence Street until you reach the second house on your right.

STOP 6:
THE JOHN SEABROOK HOUSE,
47 LAWRENCE STREET

This home was built in the 1850s by John Archibald Seabrook, a planter from Edisto Island. He bought the Foot Point Plantation in 1853. This house was one of nine that survived the burning of Bluffton.

This house was one of nine that survived the June 1863 burning of Bluffton.

Retrace your steps back towards Calhoun Street, cross it and continue on Lawrence Street, traveling in an easterly direction. Make a right onto Boundary Street, follow this street while crossing Green Street, stop at the house on the corner.

STOP 7:
THE HEYWARD HOUSE,
70 BOUNDARY STREET

This home was built in 1840 as summer house for John James Cole, a local planter. It survived the torching of Bluffton in June 1863. It was purchased by the Heyward family after the Civil War. Today it is the Official Welcome Center for Bluffton and the headquarters of the Bluffton Historical Preservation Society. Tours are available.

The home is open Monday – Friday from 10:00 a.m. to 3:00 p.m. Saturday 11:00 a.m. – 2:00 p.m.
(843) 757-6293
www.heywardhouse.org

The Official Welcome Center for Bluffton, the Heyward House.

Slave quarters of the Heyward House.

The interior of a slave's quarters.

Continue down Boundary Street, turn left onto Bridge Street, stop at the first house on your left.

STOP 8:
THE FRIPP HOUSE,
48 BRIDGE STREET

This home was built in 1835 and was a residence for the Fripp family, one of the leading cotton planters in the area. The Fripps were one of the wealthiest planter families in South Carolina; they also owned many homes in Beaufort. This home survived the burning of Bluffton.

One of many homes owned by the Fripp's in the Low Country.

Continue up the street, stopping at the next house.

STOP 9:
THE CARD HOUSE,
34 BRIDGE STREET

This home was built in 1825. It was used as summer home for a local family and saw many poker games; the most famous poker game occurred in 1837, when William Baynard won the deed to Braddock's Point Plantation on Hilton Head Island. This house survived the burning of Bluffton in June 1863.

The house was known for its high stakes poker games before the war.

Retrace your steps back towards Boundary Street, cross Bridge Street to the sidewalk on the other side, in a westerly direction. Take a left onto Calhoun Street, cross Allen Street, stop at the church.

STOP 10:

BLUFFTON UNITED METHODIST CHURCH, 101 CALHOUN STREET

The original church as built in 1853; some Confederate soldiers prevented the burning of the church in 1863, when a Union raiding party set fire to a good part of Bluffton. The parsonage was destroyed; a fire was set at the altar, but burned slowly, allowing soldiers to save the church.[12] The church was destroyed by a hurricane in 1940 and was rebuilt in 1945.

Confederate troops used Bluffton as a base to raid Hilton Head and Daufuskie Islands.

Quick reacting Confederate soldiers saved the Church from Yankee fires in 1863.

Continue down Calhoun Street, stopping at the corner of Water and Calhoun Streets.

STOP 11:
SQUIRE POPE'S SUMMER
HOUSE, 111 CALHOUN STREET

This home was built in 1850 for Squire Pope, a planter on Hilton Head and Daufuskie Islands. It was destroyed on June 3, 1863, by Union troops. After the war, Mrs. Pope and her daughter returned to Bluffton; the only two structures that survived were the carriage house and another smaller building nearby. They were later joined together to form the present structure.

Union troops covering the burning of Bluffton on June 3, 1863.

This family owned cotton plantations on both Hilton Head and Daufuskie Islands.

To return to 278, follow Calhoun Street to SC 46, the May River Road, make a right. Follow 46 to the four-way stop, turn left onto 46 East, it is 1.7 miles to US 278.

Chapter 2

HILTON HEAD ISLAND TOUR, BROTHER AGAINST BROTHER, DRIVING TOUR

Before you cross the bridge onto Hilton Head Island, the area on the right was known as Buckingham Plantation. Eshriam Baynard owned this plantation; he was the son of William Baynard, who owned Braddock's Point Plantation. Eshriam also owned the Davenport house in nearby Savannah.

Before the war started, Hilton Head Island was the home of over twenty cotton plantations

As you cross over the bridge onto Hilton Head Island, drive 1.1 miles and make a right into the Coastal Discovery Museum.

STOP 1:

COASTAL DISCOVERY MUSEUM, 100 WILLIAM HILTON PARKWAY

This would be a good stop to get the layout of Hilton Head Island. There are many tours that focus on life before and during the war: a Civil War history, the African-American experience, and life on an antebellum plantation guided tours.

The museum is open Monday through Saturday from 9:00 a.m. to 5:00 p.m. It is open on Sunday, 10:00 a.m. to 2:00 p.m.
843-689-6767
www.coastaldiscovery.org

A field piece at the museum.

From the parking lot turn right onto US 278 East, get in the left lane. Drive onto the Cross Island Parkway, it is a toll road; after passing the tollbooth, switch into the right lane. You are now traveling on Palmetto Bay Road; turn right into the traffic circle, stay in the right lane, and make the first exit off the circle. You are now entering Sea Pines; you will need to pay for a pass to enter. You are now on Greenwood Drive; travel 2.6 miles to the traffic circle, exit to the right onto Plantation Drive for .5 miles, and then turn left onto Lighthouse Road. Continue on this road for .7 miles and pull off into the parking lot on your right. You will need to use the trails to visit the ruins.

STOP 2:
BRADDOCK'S POINT PLANTATION (STONEY – BAYNARD RUINS, SEA PINES)

The ruins are remnants of an antebellum plantation home built between 1793-1820 by Captain John Stoney. It was constructed of timber and tabby. Tabby is a mixture of oyster shells, lime, and sand that was used in construction throughout the Low Country.

In 1837, the Stoney family declared bankruptcy, so William Baynard obtained the property from a game of poker that was played at Bluffton's "card house."[13] Before the invasion, a Confederate battery was positioned nearby to help protect this part of Hilton Head Island. It was raided by Union troops after the occupation of Hilton Head in November 1861. It was later used as Headquarters for the Union forces stationed on the island. The home burned after the war.

Ruins of the exterior of the main house at Braddock's Point.

Interior of the main house.

Foundation ruins
of slave quarters at
Braddock's Point.

Slaves outside their quarters from the Low
Country. *Courtesy of the Library of Congress.*

Retrace your route by returning to Plantation Road, .7 miles from the ruins. Turn right onto Plantation Drive for .5 miles; follow the circle to the third exit to Greenwood Drive. You will travel 2.6 miles back to the Sea Pines Circle. When entering the circle, make the second right on US 278 Business West. Travel west through four stoplights, 5 miles, make a right at the fifth light onto Folly Field Road. Follow the road all the way down to the beach parking. Exit your vehicle and walk the ramp to the beach; look to your left at Port Royal Sound.

STOP 3:

FORT WALKER,

NEAR FOLLY FIELD BEACH

"I am of the opinion that the entrance to the magnificent and impor-tant harbor of Port Royal can be effectually protected by two strong works on Hilton Head and Bay Point, on each side of the entrance, and a steel clad floating battery moored halfway between the two. All armed with the heaviest rifled guns that can be made, but the construction not being practicable at present, I have resorted to local works."[14]

General Pierre Beauregard's statement,
made while touring the area on May 16, 1861;
but, it was decided that Charleston's defense
was the top priority.

The remains of this fort are actually in Port Royal Plantation, but access is not readily available, so we are in the vicinity where the Union landings occurred.

Construction began on the fort in July 1861. Island planters furnished slave labor that hauled Palmetto logs, dug trenches, erected a powder magazine, and constructed gun emplacements.[15] Another fort was constructed three miles across Port Royal Sound, Fort Beauregard at Bay Point. This battery was named Fort Walker, in honor of the Confederate Secretary of War, L. P. Walker. It was hoped that perhaps Walker would secure additional artillery to help protect his namesake. By November, the fort was armed with one ten-inch Columbiad, an eight-inch Columbiad, a 24 pounder, and nine Navy 32 pounders.[16] The garrison consisted of the 11th South Carolina Infantry and the German Artillery of Charleston.[17]

Confederate General Thomas Drayton was informed on November 1, six days before the landings, that an attack was imminent on the island.[18] He arrived three days later to oversee the defenses of Hilton Head Island.

The Federal fleets arrived on November 4, 1861, near the bar of Port Royal Sound and were met by Confederate Admiral Josiah Tattnall's mosquito fleet, the *Savannah*, the *Sampson,* and the *Resolute.* Additional

Remains of Fort Walker today in Port Royal Plantation.

Fort Walker after capture by Union forces. *Courtesy of the Library of Congress*.

34

ships, the *Huntress* and the *Lady Davis* from Beaufort, later joined Tattnall's force.[19] They engaged the enemy, but did not have the range or the armament to fully challenge the Yankee force. They withdrew to the protection of Skull Creek during the bombardment of the forts. A small landing party from these vessels tried to bring additional munitions, but the fort had been abandoned before they arrived. The Union navy attacked on an elliptical path, firing on both Forts Walker and Beauregard; they had massed 155 guns on November 7.[20]

Federal troops later landed and overpowered Fort Walker on Squire Pope's Coggon's Point Plantation, despite the reinforcements of 450 Georgia infantry that had been dispatched from Savannah.[21] The battery was abandoned before reinforcements, a small band of Confederate States Marines, could arrive, but they later helped cover the retreat while skirmishing with Federal Marines.[22] Fort Gilmore was later built by Union forces near this area.

Later tradesmen descended upon this area, building hotels, bars, photography studios, barber shops, drug stores, dry good stores, and shoe stores. They were called Sutlers, but the Union troops called the area "Robber's Row," the name of the golf course in Port Royal Plantation.

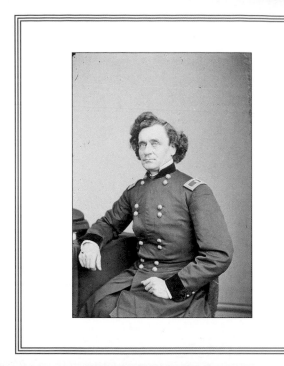

Brigadier General Thomas Sherman, who led the attack on Hilton Head. *Courtesy of the Library of Congress.*

Confederate troops defending Fort Walker against amphibious assault.

Interior of Fort Walker, held by Southern infantry.

Union troops advancing towards Fort Walker.

Folly Field beach, near where the Federal landings occurred.

Retrace your route back to US 278 and turn right. Travel through two stoplights and turn right at the third light onto Matthews Drive, for .7 miles. Turn right on to Beach City Road; drive 1.2 miles to the intersection with Fish Haul Road.

STOP 4:

MITCHELLVILLE

"Negroes slaves came flocking into our camp by the hundreds, escaping their masters when they knew of the landings of 'Lincoln soldiers' as they called us...many with no other clothing than gunnysacks,"
remarked a Union soldier, observing the number of slaves that flocked to the occupation forces.[23]

Almost immediately after the Union occupation, almost five hundred slaves took refuge on Hilton Head. Mitchellville was laid out on a cotton field that was part of the Fish Haul Plantation. It was divided into one-quarter lots; there were elected officials, schools, shops, clinics, a church, kitchens, and homes for the former slaves to live in as they raised cotton for Union use. Children between the ages of six and fifteen were required to attend school. Government sawmills turned out pine siding to build these structures. Treasury agents had hired these crews to bring in the Sea Island cotton. By November of 1865, Mitchellville had 1,500 residents and the town ceased to exist in 1868 after the army left Hilton Head.

General Hunter, after losing troops to McCellan's army in Virginia, asked Washington to raise regiments of African-Americans to increase his strength. He was authorized to raise 5,000.[24] Many of these regiments were raised during the winter of 1863-64.

Freedmen's Aid Society did educational work here and in the surrounding area.

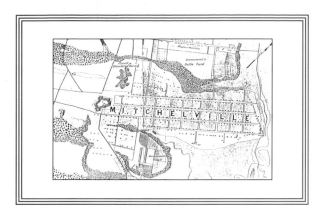

Mitchellville, the first African-American town on
Hilton Head Island.

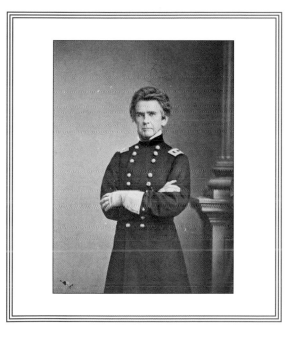

Brigadier General Ormsby Mitchell,
organized Mitchellville.

Site where Mitchellville once stood.

*Make a left on to Fish Haul Road, .5 miles. Turn right on to Buygall
Road; stop at the baseball field. You are now at the area that made up
Fish Haul Plantation.*

STOP 5:

FISH HAUL PLANTATION RUINS

This cotton plantation was owned by Confederate General Thomas F. Drayton, whose wife, Catherine Pope, had inherited Fish Haul Plantation.[25] Drayton was a planter and a close friend to President Davis.[26] He had graduated from West Point in 1828; he was also a proponent for states' rights. After the evacuation of Hilton Head, Drayton led a brigade with the Army of Northern Virginia until the Battle of Sharpsburg. He was later transferred to General Sterling Price's Confederate army in Missouri. He died in Florence, South Carolina, in 1891.

Percival Drayton, Thomas Drayton's brother, had made his decision to continue to serve with the United States' Navy without grasping the cost of his choice when the war began. Percival was born in 1812 and was appointed a navy midshipman in 1827. Captain Drayton had been stationed at the Philadelphia Naval Yard in April 1861 and after the firing on Fort Sumter had his status as a citizen of South Carolina removed from the naval records. Percival and Thomas met for the last time in early 1861 at Charleston's St. Michael's Church; they prayed together all night and then went their separate ways, never setting eyes on each other again.[27]

Slaves from Fish Haul Plantation.
Courtesy of the Library of Congress.

Percival was part of the invasion against Port Royal Sound; he knew the importance of Hilton Head Island as a base for the blockading Federal fleet. His brother Thomas and friends were waiting for him on Hilton Head.[28] He was later involved in shore operations along the South Carolina, Georgia, and Florida coasts, including some of the attacks against Fort McAllister in Savannah. Percival was promoted to Fleet Captain of the West Gulf Blockading Squadron, leading it into action in the Battle of Mobile Bay in August 1864. He would die of sickness at Washington on August 4, 1865.

Ruins of slave quarters from Fish Haul Plantation.

Retrace your drive onto Fish Haul Road, travel .5 miles back to Beach City Road, turn right. Travel .1 mile to Fort Howell on your right.

STOP 6:
FORT HOWELL RUINS

On September 26, 1864, Major General John G. Foster, commander of the Department of the South, ordered the construction of this fort.[29] The fort's earthworks were designed to protect Mitchellville, and covered three acres of land. Soldiers of the 32nd United States' Colored Infantry built Fort Howell on the plantation grounds of Captain William Pope. The fort was named for Union General Joshua B. Howell, commander of the 3rd Division of the X Corps. Howell was fifty-eight when he died from injuries he suffered after falling off his horse at X Corps Headquarters at Petersburg in September 1864. The fort was protected by four guns.

Union troops in camp around Hilton Head Island.

Return to Beach City Road and drive 1.5 miles to US 278 West. Turn right and travel through two lights. After passing the second light, get in the far right lane and turn right at the next light on to Gumtree Road, .6 miles. Travel 1.4 miles to the intersection with Squire Pope Road, turn right. Drive .4 miles to the back gate of Hilton Head Plantation. Tell the security guard you are going to the Old Fort Pub. After passing the gate, travel .3 miles and turn left on to Skull Creek Drive and then turn left into the Old Fort Pub parking lot.

Remnants of Fort Howell, which protected Mitchellville from Confederate attacks.

Around this area was the Coggins Point Plantation, today Port Royal Plantation. Federals landed in this location after the fall of Fort Walker on November 7, 1861. They were pressing the Confederates to the north end of Hilton Head Island. A signal tower was later built on the Pope House, so that General Hunter and Admiral DuPont could communicate. They were suppose to concentrate all their efforts by using Hilton Head as a base to capture the Charleston and Savannah Railroad, but the two argued and they never moved against the line.[30]

STOP 7:

FORT MITCHELL RUINS –

HILTON HEAD PLANTATION

On December 6, 1861, a Confederate raiding party was led by local boys, John and Rollin Kirk, against the cotton fields and structures along Skull Creek.[31] They got away with boat loads of food and some of their former slaves. This fort was constructed to protect Hilton Head from further Confederate raids.

The fort was named for Union Major General Ormsby Mitchell; it protected Skull Creek from a possible Confederate naval attack from Savannah. The earthworks protected the north end of Hilton Head Island; the attack never came and the guns never fired a shot in anger. The earthworks had up to six guns that were aimed at Skull Creek. It was thought that a Confederate invasion was possible from Bluffton.

Earlier in the war, Mitchell had captured Huntsville, Alabama, during The Great Locomotive Chase. Union spies tried to rip up the rail line between Atlanta and Chattanooga in early April 1862. Later, Mitchell became the commander of the Department of the South, he tried to cut the Charleston and Savannah Railroad in October 1862, but Confederate reinforcements forced his withdrawal.[32] He died at the end of October in Beaufort from complications of Yellow Fever; he was fifty-six years old.

The CSS *Atlanta,* an ironclad based in Savannah, was commanded by Commander W. A. Webb, who planned to break the blockade between Savannah and Charleston by attacking the Federal installation at Hilton Head. Confederate naval authorities thought a raid by ironclads could break the blockade, but in reality they were unable to perform in rough sea waters. An attempt was made on June 17, 1863, but the *Atlanta* ran aground near Savannah and was captured.[33]

Remains of the west wall of Fort Mitchell.

Left:
The east wall of Fort Mitchell, built in 1862.

Fort Mitchell protected Hilton Head from any Confederate raids that came from Bluffton.

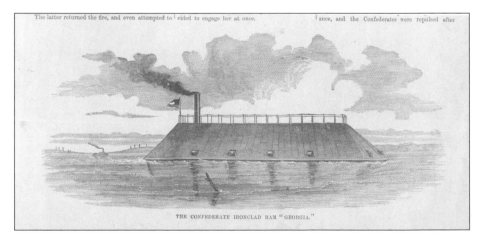

It was feared the Confederate ironclads from Savannah would attack Fort Mitchell. *Courtesy of the Coastal Heritage Society.*

Many women spent time with their husbands while they were assigned to Hilton Head.

Return the same way you came, through the back gate of Hilton Head Plantation; stay on Squire Pope Road until it intersects with US 278 West, 1.6 miles. Turn right onto US 278 West to Pinckney Island and make the first right after crossing the first bridge. You are now entering the Pinckney Island National Refuge.

STOP 8:
PINCKNEY ISLAND

A cotton plantation and mansion occupied the island before the war, but the mansion house had been destroyed by a hurricane around 1859.[34] A half a million dollars of cotton was sent to New York from the captured Sea Islands in the seven months that followed the fall of Hilton Head Island.[35]

Elements of the 3rd New Hampshire Infantry occupied the island in July 1862, but many of the men became sick and were ordered back to Hilton Head Island.[36] On August 20, 1862, Captain Stephen Elliot, whose family had property confiscated here, led about 200 men of the 11th South Carolina Infantry to this island and captured the Federal pickets. Elliot had raided this area before in an effort to destroy the cotton that was being grown by the Federals on the island and burned some of the remaining structures.[37] The island was later sold for taxes levied against it during the war.

Confederates raiders frequently occupied Pinckney Island in 1862.

The next stop is Parris Island, on the way to Beaufort. Follow US 278 West and turn right onto SC 170 East towards Beaufort. Travel 14.5 miles on 170. Turn right onto SC 802 East to Parris Island, travel 3.5 miles. Obtain a pass from the sentries to visit the museum on Parris Island. As you enter the island, stop at the visitor's center to obtain a map of the island.

As you drive on SC 170 you will pass Oldfield Plantation, a housing development today. In 1862, Union gunboats operating on the Okatie River destroyed the plantation home.

STOP 9:

PARRIS ISLAND

The surrounding harbor was used as the United States' Navy Headquarters of the South Atlantic Blockading Fleet. The museum has a nice collection of Civil War artifacts and interpretation of the Low Country's military history.

Open daily, 10:00 a.m. – 4:30 p.m.
843-228-2166
www.pimuseum.us

Retrace your way back to 802, turn right towards Beaufort. Drive into historic Beaufort.

Chapter 3

THE SECESSION MOVEMENT & OCCUPATION OF BEAUFORT WALKING TOUR

Beaufort was occupied by General Isaac Stevens's Brigade on December 11, 1861. The force consisted of the 100th Pennsylvania Infantry, 79th New York Highlanders, 8th Michigan Infantry, and Battery E of the United States 3rd Artillery. The planters and most townspeople escaped, and the unsupervised slaves looted the town before Stevens arrived.[38]

Start your tour from the parking lot at the city marina. From the marina walk towards Bay Street and turn right, walk down to the intersection with West Street, turn left onto West Street. Follow West Street until it intersects with Craven Street, turn left. Stop at 901 Craven, on the corner.

STOP 1:

W. J. JENKINS HOME, 901 CRAVEN STREET

"Nearly all the houses in Beaufort have a dismantled, desolate look. Few persons are to be seen in the streets, some soldiers and contrabands. I believe we saw only three ladies,"
Charlotte Forten, a visiting schoolteacher from New England, was remarking how deserted Beaufort looked in early 1863.[39]

This home was built in 1845; during the occupation many homes like this had property taken and much was shipped up North by Union officers who labeled it as personal baggage.

The W. J. Jenkins house was built in 1845.

Continue down Craven Street and stop at the church on the corner with Charles street.

STOP 2:
TABERNACLE BAPTIST CHURCH, 911 CRAVEN STREET

The church was built in 1845; originally it was owned by the Baptist Church of Beaufort and used as an evening meeting house. In 1856, the congregation had well over 3,000 parishioners, with over ninety percent made up of slaves. Most slaves were unable to attend services, so they worshiped in chapels on the plantations. During the war, freed slaves purchased and established the church for their use. Robert Smalls and his family are buried in the yard to your right.

Tabernacle Church was opened as a African-American church in 1863.

Robert Smalls was born a slave and later served in Congress.

Turn right onto Charles Street, cross to the other side of the street, and continue until it intersects with King Street.

STOP 3:
BAPTIST CHURCH OF BEAUFORT

"The churches were robbed of all ornament. The keys torn from the organs to make letters for their caps and even the brick wall enclosing the dead was torn away from a chimney..."

**Dr. Esther Hill Hawks, a Physician,
remarking about the vandalism on October 16, 1862.**[40]

The church was organized in 1804 and the current structure was built in 1844. During the war years, many items went missing and it was used as a hospital for Union African-American soldiers during the occupation of Beaufort. The steeple was a later addition after the war and just recently the church went through a major renovation. The church is open during the week for visitation.

www.bcob.org

The church was built in 1844 and served as a hospital during the war.

Retrace your steps down Charles Street and turn right onto Craven Street; stop at the house at the intersection with Newcastle Street.

STOP 4:

THOMAS RHETT HOUSE INN, 1009 CRAVEN STREET

This house was built in 1820, Rhett's brothers Edmund and Robert were staunch leaders in the South Carolina secessionist movement. Today it is a Bed and Breakfast.

This home was built in 1820 and is now a Bed & Breakfast.

Continue down Craven.

STOP 5:
WILLIAM FICKLING HOUSE,
1109 CRAVEN STREET

This home was built in the early 1800s. Its elevation was designed to allow the flow of air through the home to cool it during the warmer months.

This antebellum home was built in the early 1800s.

Continue on Craven and stop at the next house on the right.

STOP 6:
MILTON MAXCY HOUSE,
"SECESSION HOUSE,"
1113 CRAVEN STREET

"On the 20th of December an ordinance was passed declaring her (South Carolina) connection with the Union forever severed...What was done in Beaufort? Here upon receipt of intelligence that the ordinance had passed in the convention, the excitement was wild; bonfires were kindled, night processions were made with transparencies revealing select political maxims, and numerous other demonstrations of satisfaction and joy. Many believed that the separation would be peaceful,"

Doctor John Archibald Johnson, who witnessed the secession celebrations in Beaufort.[41]

This house was built around 1813. The house got its nickname, Secession House, because of the influence of Robert Barnwell Rhett, a United States Senator from South Carolina, who strongly advocated secession.

Many secession speeches were given here before South Carolina seceded.

Many meetings on the subject took place here. In December 1860, delegates to the Charleston Convention left this house for a nearby boat landing in order to attend the convention in Charleston. Rhett had later hoped, while attending the Confederate Convention at Montgomery, Alabama, in February 1861, to be elected President of the Confederacy, but instead waged a political campaign against President Jefferson Davis throughout the war.

The house was occupied by Union forces and later the United States' Tax Commission took possession of it. It was the headquarters of General Rufus Saxon during the occupation of Beaufort. The house was returned to the family after the war, after the payment of the taxes.[42]

Cross Church Street and turn left. Once on Bay Street, turn right.

STOP 7:
CUTHBERT HOUSE INN,
1203 BAY STREET

This home was built in 1810. At the start of the war, it was the home of Mary Cuthbert Stuart and her daughter. She fled Beaufort when Hilton Head was invaded and never returned. The house was confiscated and purchased by General Rufus Saxton, the military governor of the Sea Islands. Saxton was born in Massachusetts in 1824 and graduated West Point in 1849. Early in the war, he commanded the Union defenses at Harper's Ferry. After the war, Saxton served in the Quarter Masters Corps until he retired in 1888. He was awarded the Congressional Medal of Honor in 1893 and died in 1908. He is buried at Arlington National Cemetery. On January 23, 1865, General William T. Sherman stayed here one night, as a guest of General Saxton.[43] It is now a Bed and Breakfast.

Today the Cuthbert house serves as a Bed & Breakfast.

This home was built in 1810 and was abandoned in November 1861.

Great view of the Beaufort River from one of the front rooms.

Right:
A main sitting room in
the Cuthbert House.

Continue along Bay Street, stop at the next house.

STOP 8:
ROBERT MEANS HOUSE, 1207 BAY STREET

This home was built in 1790. In 1864, it was the home of Captain Joseph Lowe, the Army Quartermaster.[44] Lowe was in charge of issuing equipment to the Union soldiers in the Beaufort area.

During the war, this house was the residence of the Union Army Quartermaster.

Continue along Bay Street, stopping two houses down.

STOP 9:
THOMAS FULLER HOUSE, 1211 BAY STREET

This house was built in 1796; it is unique because much of the building material is tabby. Tabby is a form of concrete mixed with lime, sand, water, and oyster shells.

One of the early antebellum homes found on Bay Street.

Continue on Bay, crossing Harrington Street, stop at the corner.

STOP 10:
CHARLES H. LEVERE HOUSE, 1301 BAY

This home was built before the Revolutionary War. Its location allowed the house to take advantage of the breeze coming off the water.

This house was built before the Revolutionary War.

Continue along Bay, crossing Wilmington Street, stop at the corner.

STOP 11:
JOHN JOYNER SMITH HOUSE

"We are now pleasantly living in Beaufort with all sorts of comforts at our disposal. The original house occupied by General Stevens is the one belonging to Mr. Smith and is an extremely elegant one. The portrait of Bishop Elliot looks down benignly from the mantle while I write. I wish the owners were back in their homes."

**William Lusk, a member of General
Isaac Stevens' Staff in early 1862.**[45]

This home was built in 1811. In 1861, John Smith was a wealthy and prominent citizen, serving the Confederate cause. Smith had his house confiscated by the Federal government through the newly created tax act.[46] General Stevens occupied this house while assigned to command an infantry brigade at Beaufort in the Spring of 1862.

General Isaac Stevens resided here in 1862 while looking for ways to cut the Charleston & Savannah Railroad.

General Stevens and staff posing on the front porch of the Johnson House. *Courtesy of the Library of Congress.*

Continue on Bay Street, stop at the next house.

STOP 12:

EDWARD BARNWELL HOUSE, 1405 BAY STREET

"In regard to danger of sickness,... the planters generally went to Beaufort... the summer was the fashionable and social time here, when the rich people lived together, gave parties, etc."

William C. Gannett visiting from the North in June 1862.[47]

This house most likely was occupied by Union troops.

This house saw a great many social gatherings during "social seasons" before the war.

Continue on Bay Street, cross Manson Street, stop at the monument in front of the court house.

STOP 13:

UNITED STATES DISTRICT
COURT, SITE OF THE CASTLE

The monument honors Confederate dead; it was erected by the Stephen Elliot Chapter of the United Daughters of the Confederacy.

On this site was the home, the Castle, of Robert Woodward Barnwell, a planter, lawyer, and educator. He was born in Beaufort in 1801; he attended Beaufort College and Harvard. In 1826, he was elected to the South Carolina House of Representatives; two years later he was elected to Congress. He served until 1833, declining a bid for reelection.

This is a monument to the Confederate dead.

From 1833 to 1841, he served as the President of South Carolina College, presently the University of South Carolina. In 1850, Barnwell was appointed to the United States Senate after the passing of Franklin Elmore; he served only six months. Robert Barnwell Rhett then was elected to the office.

Barnwell was a delegate to the Provisional Confederate Congress; he cast a vote on February 9, 1861, that ensured the election of Jefferson Davis to the Confederate Presidency. Throughout the war he represented South Carolina in the Confederate Senate in Richmond. After the war he would return to the University of South Carolina; a college in Columbia is named after him.

Barnwell's son, Robert Jr., graduated South Carolina College and later became the chaplain of that school. At the start of the war, Robert Jr. helped organize South Carolina hospitals. He later worked in hospitals in Virginia.[48]

Turn right onto North Street, walk four blocks to corner of North and Church Streets.

STOP 14:
ST. HELENA'S EPISCOPAL CHURCH, 505 CHURCH STREET

"God Save the South. God was nigh to all who called upon him. Gather their households together and hold family prayers..."
Dr. Walker preached that the Lord would deliver the town of Beaufort from the Yankee invader, November 3, 1861.[49]

The church was built in 1817 and was enlarged in 1842. The steeple was taken down in 1860 because it was teetering in the wind; it was not replaced until World War II. The cemetery is the resting place of many Confederate soldiers, including two generals, Lt. General Robert H. Anderson and Brigadier General Stephen Elliot. On the Sunday before the Union attack on Hilton Head Island, the congregation knew an invasion was imminent. They were given instructions to leave Beaufort if they heard the bells ring at noon, giving advance notice to allow them to escape.[50] The church was used as a hospital during the war; marble headstones were used to operate on. Those types of headstones were used because they were easier to keep sterile for surgery. Names of thirty-three parishioners that died in the service of the Confederate armies are placed on an interior wall.

St. Helena's Episcopal Church lost over forty parishioners who served the Confederacy during the war.

Headstone of Lieutenant Richard H. Anderson, one of Lee's corps commanders.

Burial site of Brigadier General Stephen Elliot.

Turn around and turn left onto Church Street, cross onto the right side. Turn left onto Bay Street. The marina is directly in front of you as you approach Bay Street. Stop at the intersection with Newcastle, stopping at the house on the corner.

STOP 15:
WILLIAM ELLIOTT HOUSE,
"ANCHORAGE HOUSE,"
1001 BAY STREET

This home was built in 1770. Stephen Elliott's father had introduced Sea Island cotton to South Carolina. The house was used as a hospital during the Union occupation.

A fiery speech was made from it's balcony by General Wade Hampton during the Red Shirt Campaign. The "Red Shirt Campaign" by Wade Hampton in 1876 was designed to further erode the few freedoms still held by African-Americans. The campaign document directs, in part: "In speeches to negroes you must remember that argument has no effect upon them: they can only be influenced by their fears, superstition and cupidity. Do not attempt to flatter and persuade them. ... Treat them so as to show them you are the superior race, and that their natural position is that of subordination to the white man."[51]

This home was built in 1770 and was home to the Elliot family.

Continue on Bay Street towards downtown. Turn left onto Charles Street and turn right onto Port Republic Street, cross the street.

STOP 16:

LOCUS CUTHBERT HOUSE, 915 PORT REPUBLIC STREET

This home was built in 1820. This family also was one of Beaufort's wealthiest.

Another house owned by the Cuthbert family. This house was built in 1820.

Turn around and retrace your steps back to Bay Street.

Tour Ends

Chapter 4

CONFEDERATE OFFICERS AND PLANTERS WALKING TOUR

From the Waterfront Park, turn right onto Bay Street and continue walking east. Once you cross Carteret Street, stop at the two cannons.

STOP 1:

BRIGADIER GENERAL STEPHEN ELLIOT MONUMENT

"Their boats were broken by grenades and masses of masonry and bricks and our muskets would keep popping them over and in pairs and squads they quietly walked round and surrendered to their perfect amazement,"
Lieutenant Colonel Stephen Elliot recounting the failure of the Federal amphibious assault on Fort Sumter, September 8, 1863.[52]

Stephen Elliot was born at Beaufort on October 26, 1830. At the start of the war he organized a light battery, the Beaufort Artillery. Elliot and some of the unit took part in the shelling of Fort Sumter on April 12, 1861. Later he was ordered to Bay Point, Fort Beauregard, engaging the Federal fleet for two hours as it attacked the forts in Port Royal Sound on November 7, 1861.

After the fall of the coastal islands, Elliot and others based in Bluffton raided Pinckney and Hilton Head Islands by burning plantation homes and fields. For his success he was promoted chief of artillery of the Third Military District, which included Beaufort. He also developed the sunken torpedo. Twice he helped defend against Yankee attempts to cut the Charleston and Savannah Railroad at Pocotaligo. In September 1863 he was placed in command of Fort Sumter and remained there until May 1864.

That spring he was ordered to join the Army of Northern Virginia. Two of his regiments, the 18th and 22nd South Carolina Infantry, were in the area where the mine exploded on June 30, 1864, at Petersburg. During the Battle of the Crater, he helped defend the salient and later led a counterattack that led to his wounding, which took him out of action for some time. During Sherman's invasion of North Carolina, he led a brigade that opposed the invaders at Bentonville in March 1865, where he received another wound. He would succumb to his wounds at Beaufort on March 21, 1866.

This monument is to Confederate General Stephen Elliot, whose house once faced the river before the fire of 1907.

Cross to the other side of the street, stop at the house on the corner.

STOP 2:
LEWIS REEVE SAMS HOUSE,
601 BAY STREET

This house was built in 1852. The home was also used as a Union hospital during the war. It was one of the few homes in the area that survived the fire of 1907.

This home was built in 1852 and was used as a hospital during the war.

Turn left onto New Street; stop at the corner. Turn right onto Port Republic Street, by crossing the street. Continue down Port Republic Street; stop at the house on the corner.

STOP 3: GEORGE MOSSE STONEY HOUSE, 500 PORT REPUBLIC STREET

This home was built in 1823 and survived the Union occupation. This family lost a son during the Battle of Bentonville, North Carolina, in March 1865.

The Stoney family lost a nineteen-year-old son at the Battle of Bentonville, North Carolina, a month before the war ended.

Turn back around, heading back to the intersection, turn left onto New Street by crossing it.

STOP 4:

BERNERS BARNWELL SAMS HOUSE, 310 NEW STREET

"Well...I'd go to the hospital; I would, early eb'ry morning! I'd get a big chunk of ice; I would and put it in a basin, and fill it with water, den I'd take a sponge and begin. Fust man I'd come to, I'd thrash away de flies, and dey'd rise, dey would, like bees roun' a hive. Den I'd begin to bathe der wounds an' by de time I'd bathed off three or four, de fire and heat would have melted de ice,"

Harriet Tubman explaining conditions while working as a nurse in Beaufort.[53]

This home was built in 1818. During the war this was General Hospital Number Ten. It's patients were African-American soldiers, the first hospital sanctioned by the War Department. Harriet Tubman made a living during the war by working in a bakery; she also helped guide Union raids up the Combahee River and volunteered to help in the hospitals.

This house was built in 1818 and also served as a hospital during the war.

Continue up New Street, turn right onto Craven Street. Cross East Street through the dead end, stop at the house on your left.

STOP 5:

JOSEPH JOHNSON HOUSE, 411 CRAVEN STREET

This antebellum house was built in 1850. The oak tree in the front yard was towering in 1861 and the owners of the house, the Johnsons, tried to escape with their belongings after Hilton Head fell. Time and lack of mobility prevented them from taking much, so they buried some of the expensive items in the ground beneath an outhouse.

After the war, Joseph Johnson returned to Beaufort, learning that his home was occupied and was up for sale because of unpaid back taxes. One dark night he was able, without any alarm, to find his items that he buried. He promptly sold them and paid the taxes to reacquire his home.

This antebellum home was built in 1850.

Turn around and make a right onto East Street. Continue north on East Street; turn right onto the next street, Federal. Stop at the house on the corner.

STOP 6:

AN ANTEBELLUM HOUSE

"Our planters, with few exceptions, were accustomed to hail the first appearance of frost as the time for removing from town, to their plantations,"

Doctor John Archibald Johnson noting that the planters would return to their plantation residences when the threat of fever diminished.[54]

This home was used as a summer house for a local family to escape the heat and threat of fever; the home was occupied from mid-May through mid-November during the year.

This antebellum home was a summer residence for a local family before the war.

Continue east on Federal Street, cross Hamilton Street, stopping at the next house on the left after crossing the street.

STOP 7:
JOHN BLYTHEWOOD HOUSE,
315 FEDERAL STREET

"When the troops from Bay Point, including...the Beaufort Artillery, reached town on Friday, they found it, already, almost deserted. Lieutenant Johnson had remained on the island, directing the transportation to St. Helena, until after midnight...and, with T. B. Chaplin, had returned to Trenchard's Inlet, before day dawn, in search of exhausted and missing men. He did not reach Beaufort till sunset on Friday. Landing at the foot of Carteret Street, he looked in vain for one living creature, human or other, throughout the length of Bay Street. Walking up as far as the arsenal, and then turning down Craven, to East Street, he did not meet one person until he had nearly reached the bridge on Federal Alley. There he encountered two German mechanics, who informed him of the time and manner of the citizen's departure. They also were just about to leave, on foot,"

Doctor John A. Johnson on how the citizens evacuated Beaufort after the fall of forts Walker and Beauregard.[55]

This home was built in the 1800s and survived the war.

The John Bythewood House, another antebellum home that survived the war.

Continue on Federal Street, stop at the last house on the right.

STOP 8:
WILLIAM FRIPP HOUSE,
302 FEDERAL STREET

This home was built in 1832 and was one of many homes owned by the Fripp family, including some property in Bluffton.

This home was built in 1832 by the wealthy Fripp family.

Continue to the end of the street.

STOP 9:
JAMES ROBERT VERDIER
HOUSE, MARSHLANDS,
501 PINCKNEY STREET

This home was built in 1814. During the war it was used by the United States Sanitary Commission; many of the wounded and sick were from the coastal areas of South Carolina, Georgia, and Florida were brought through here for medical care.

"Marshlands" was built in 1814 and used as a hospital during the war.

Turn left onto Pinckney Street, walk and turn left onto King Street. Stop at the house on the corner.

STOP 10:
EDWARD MEANS HOUSE,
INTERSECTION OF KING AND
PINCKNEY STREETS

"The splendor of the houses and furniture and the beauty may have been exaggerated, but the house of Colonel Edward Means would be called handsome in any town in the North,"

a visiting Northern war correspondent in December 1861.[56]

This home was built in 1853.

The Edward Means House was built in 1853.

Turn around and walk down King Street, turn left onto Short Street.

STOP 11:
PAUL HAMILTON HOUSE, "THE OAKS," THE CORNER OF KING AND SHORT STREETS

The family lost a son during the war; he had ridden with General Wade Hampton's cavalry. After the war, the Hamilton's were destitute and could not pay the taxes; neighbors pooled their resources, paying the back taxes and deeding the property back to the Hamiltons.

The Hamilton family lost a son that rode with Wade Hampton's Confederate cavalry late in the war.

Continue up Short Street, turn right onto Laurens Street, stop at the last house on the left.

STOP 12:
EDGAR FRIPP HOUSE,
1 LAURENS STREET

This home was built in 1856 and was owned by one of the wealthiest planter families in the Low Country. This home was later sold to his brother, James, who at the end of the war had no means to pay the back taxes. A French visitor, sympathetic to the South, paid the taxes and turned the title over to James Fripp. Fripp was never able to repay the debt, for the kind gentlemen returned to France.

This home was built in 1856 for the Fripp Family.

Turn around and re-cross Short Street.

STOP 13:
BERNERS BARNWELL SAMS HOUSE # 2,
201 LAURENS STREET

This home was built in 1852. Before the war, the house was the site of many parties attended by local planters and their families. During the war, it served as a Union hospital.

This home was built in 1852 and served as a hospital during the war.

Turn around, turn left onto Short Street, then turn left onto Hancock Street.

STOP 14:
FRANCIS HEXT HOUSE,
207 HANCOCK STREET

This home was built in 1720 and is one of the oldest structures in Beaufort.

This is one of the oldest homes in Beaufort, built in 1720.

Continue walking west on Hancock Street, crossing Pinckney Street. Stop at the house on the corner of Hancock and Pinckney.

STOP 15:
JOHN A. JOHNSON HOUSE

This home was built 1850. Doctor Johnson penned a diary about life before and during the Civil War in Beaufort.

This home was built in 1850. Doctor Johnson kept a diary of his experience during the occupation of Beaufort.

Continue on Hancock Street, stop, turn left onto Hamilton Street, walk and turn right onto King Street.

STOP 16:
WILLIAM WIGG BARNWELL
HOUSE, 501 KING STREET

"As soon after dark as you can effect it, withdraw Longstreet's Corps from our lines, as quietly as possible, so that the movements will not be discovered by the enemy. When you have done this, march the troops a little way to the rear and let them have some sleep—A guide will report to you this evening. I have reason to believe the enemy is withdrawing his forces from our front, and will strike us at this point. I wish you to be there to meet him."

**General Robert E. Lee ordering
Anderson to meet the Union threat
against Spotsylvania Court House, Virginia,
on May 7, 1864.[57] Anderson kept marching
all night and beat Grant's men to Spotsylvania.**

This home was built in 1816. After the war this was the home of Confederate Lieutenant General Richard Heron Anderson. Anderson was born near Stateburg, South Carolina, on October 7, 1821. He graduated from West Point in 1842, serving with the 1st US Dragoons during the Mexican War. He resigned his commission in April 1861 and was appointed a colonel of the 1st South Carolina Infantry. Later that year, he was put in command of Charleston Harbor. Anderson was promoted to a brigadier general in July 1861 and was assigned to the Confederate army that was gathering around Richmond in February 1862. He performed well during the Peninsula Campaign and was awarded the rank of major general in July. It was his division that broke the Federal line at Second Manassas and he was wounded in the thigh at the Sunken Road during the Battle of Sharpsburg.

Right:
**This was the post-war
home of Lieutenant General
Richard H. Anderson.**

After Jackson's death, he was transferred with his division to the newly formed 3rd Corps. In May 1864, after the wounding of Longstreet during the Battle of the Wilderness, he was temporarily appointed to lead Longstreet's Corps until October. At Spotsylvania, he was credited with saving the Army of Northern Virginia, arriving before Grant could turn Lee's flank. He later was given command on the newly created 4th Corps after Longstreet's return. After the war he worked as a State Phosphate agent. He died in Beaufort on June 26, 1879.

Continue west on King Street, stop at the Church on the right.

STOP 17:
FIRST AFRICAN BAPTIST CHURCH, NEW & KING STREETS

This church opened its doors on January 1, 1865. Today it still serves as a house of prayer.

The First African Baptist Church opened its doors on January 1, 1865.

Turn left onto New Street, stop at the second house on the left.

STOP 18:
THOMAS HASELL HOUSE,
509 NORTH STREET

This home was built in 1852.

This antebellum home was built in 1852.

Continue down New Street and turn right onto Craven Street. Stop at the park on your left.

STOP 19:

UNION SQUARE

During the occupation of Beaufort, Union troops set up camps at this location.

Union Square saw many troops here, but the area was larger during the war. *Courtesy of the Library of Congress.*

Continue on Craven Street.

STOP 20:

BEAUFORT ARSENAL MUSEUM, 713 CRAVEN STREET

The original building was constructed in 1798 out of brick and tabby; it housed the Beaufort Volunteer Artillery Company. It was rebuilt in 1852 with a garrison that was capable of housing 250 men and a battery of six guns.[58] The Beaufort Artillery helped defend Fort Beauregard on November 7, 1861. Today it operates as a museum and is operated by the Historic Beaufort Foundation.

The museum is open every day except Wednesday and Sunday, 10:00 a.m. to 5:00 p.m. The museum can be reached at 843-525-7077. www.historic-beaufort.org

The Beaufort Arsenal was rebuilt in 1852 and now serves as a museum.

Continue walking down Craven Street and turn left onto Scott's Street. Stay on this street until it intersects with Bay Street. Walk over to the corner house on your right at stop.

STOP 21:

JOHN MARK VERDIER HOUSE

This home was built in 1801. Verdier was a merchant and a planter. Marquis de Lafayette visited the home in 1825 while taking a short break while traveling between Charleston and Savannah by sea. During the occupation it was used as a Post Headquarters and Adjutant General's Office for Union forces that were in Beaufort. Today it is a museum that interprets antebellum life and is operated by the Historic Beaufort Foundation.

The home is open Monday - Saturday, 10:00 a.m. to 4:00 p.m.
(843) 379-3331
www.historic-beaufort.org

The Verdier Home was built in 1801 and served as Union Army Post Headquarters and Adjutant General's Office during the occupation.

End Tour

Chapter 5

THE AFRICAN-AMERICAN EXPERIENCE & MEMORIAL WALKING TOUR

Start this tour at the Beaufort Chamber of Commerce and Visitor Center. It is located at the intersection of Boundary and Congress streets. If you drive, you can park here. Walk to Carteret Street and turn right onto Washington Street. Stop at the first house on your right.

STOP 1:

ELIZABETH GOUGH HOUSE, 705 WASHINGTON STREET

This home was built after the Revolutionary War and is one of the few structures of tabby that still survives in the Beaufort area.

The Elizabeth Gough House was built in 1786.

Turn around, cross Carteret Street, turn right, stopping at the first building on the left.

STOP 2:

BEAUFORT COLLEGE

The college was founded in 1795. The school opened its doors in 1800. They closed the doors in the fall of 1861 after the occupation by Federal troops. During the war, the school was used as a school for former slaves and as a hospital. After the war, it served as the Headquarters of the Freedman's Bureau; it later became part of the University of South Carolina.

Beaufort College, now part of the University of South Carolina, opened its doors in 1801.

Turn around, turn right onto Washington Street, cross New Street, stop at the first house on the left.

STOP 3:
CHAPLIN COURT,
507 WASHINGTON STREET

This family lost a son while he was incarcerated as a Union prisoner of war in 1865.

The Chaplin family had a son who died in a Union prison camp.

Continue on Washington, stopping at next house on the left.

STOP 4:
PETIT POINT,
503 WASHINGTON STREET

This is an antebellum home that still contains its original supporting structures.

Petit Point antebellum home.

Stop at the house in front of you.

STOP 5:
LEDBETTER HOUSE,
411 BAYNARD STREET

This house was built in the early 1800s.

This antebellum home was built in the early 1800s.

Turn right, stop at the next house.

STOP 6:

TRESCOT HOUSE

This home was built in 1860.

The Trescot House was built in 1860.

Walk down East Street, turn right onto Prince Street, stopping at the corner house on New Street.

STOP 7:

ROBERT SMALLS HOUSE OR HENRY MCKEE HOUSE, 511 PRINCE STREET

"My race needs no special defense, for the past history of them in this country proves them to be equal of any people anywhere. All they need is an equal chance in the battle of life."
Robert Smalls on November 1, 1895.

This home was built in 1834 for Henry McKee and was the boyhood home of Robert Smalls. Smalls was born a slave on April 5, 1839, in Beaufort and was owned by John McKee. McKee owned plantations on Lady's Island.

Smalls went to Charleston with McKee and secured work on the docks while working on the *Planter*. The *Planter* carried cotton from the inland plantations to Charleston and traveled along the Georgia coast. Smalls eventually was elevated to the position of a helmsman, making fifteen dollars a week. He married Hannah Jones, housemaid to a wealthy Charleston family in 1856. In 1861, the *Planter* moved militia, supplies, and weapons between Charleston, Beaufort, and Savannah, thus, allowing Smalls to learn how to navigate. The *Planter* was later assigned as the courier vessel to Brigadier General Roswell Ripley for communications with the outlaying posts. Guns were installed to protect her.[59]

On May 13, 1862, Smalls and a few followers stole the *Planter* while the officers of the vessel were at a gala at Fort Sumter. They were armed with a rifle and a pistol that were seized from the captain's cabin. They moved out into the channel while flying the Confederate and Palmetto flags, as they steamed downriver.[60] Confederate pickets ignored them as they passed Castle Pinckney and forts Johnson and Moultrie. Around sunrise they passed Fort Sumter, their flags were lowered, and a white sheet was raised as they raced towards the USS *Onward*. Upon making contact, they were directed to Hilton Head. The *Planter* was then pressed into Union naval service. Smalls was made a US Navy pilot, operating vessels between Charleston and Hilton Head. Smalls gave up valuable information about the Confederate defenses on James Island, which led to the Federal attack at Secessionville in June 1862.[61]

Smalls and his followers were awarded a bounty for turning the *Planter* over to Federal authorities; he used his reward to purchase this house through the newly created tax laws imposed during the war. After the war he was elected as a state representative and served many times in the United States Congress. He died in 1915.

Robert Smalls purchased this house with the bounty he received from stealing *The Planter.*

Continue on Prince Street.

STOP 8:
ANTEBELLUM HOUSE,
605 PRINCE STREET

Another home that survived the war.

An antebellum house
on Prince Street.

Turn around and turn left to Carteret Street, walk and make a left on Congress. Return to your car. Turn left in your car onto US 21 North; drive 1.6 miles to National Cemetery on your right. Pull in and park.

STOP 9:

UNITED STATES

NATIONAL CEMETERY

"Duty well performed...Glory and Reward Won,"
Massachusetts Governor John A. Andrew
in 1865 speech about the legacy of the
54th Massachusetts Infantry.

As you look to the left side of the cemetery, there are graves of Union soldiers that fell in the area battles or from disease. The monument in the center of the cemetery is dedicated to the Union soldiers who gave their lives. There is also a marker honoring both the 54th and 55th Massachusetts Infantry; these units both served in the Low Country throughout the war. Many of the remains of the 55th came from Folly Island, near Charleston. They were interred here in 1987.

Section 53 is the area designated for Confederate soldiers, including a monument to Lieutenant General Richard Anderson.

Outside the cemetery, there is marker for the 1st South Carolina Infantry of African Descent. This unit was formed on Hilton Head Island in May 1862. This unit participated in raids along the Georgia coast. They were later redesignated as the 33rd United States Colored Infantry and would occupy Charleston after its evacuation.

Union dead in Beaufort's National Cemetery, opened in 1863.

104

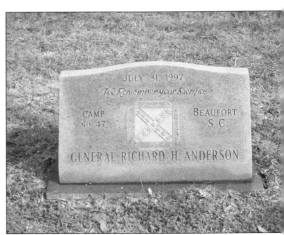

Monument to Lieutenant General Richard H. Anderson in the Confederate plot of the cemetery.

A monument to all Union Veterans that served.

This marker honors the 54th & 55th Massachusetts Infantry Regiments, which served in the Beaufort area during the war.

Honor guards today still pay respects to America's veterans.

Walk out of the cemetery and turn right; stop at the African-American Cemetery on your right.

STOP 10:

AFRICAN-AMERICAN

CEMETERY

This cemetery contains graves of the 33rd United States Colored Infantry, formerly the 1st South Carolina Infantry. Former slaves are also buried here.

Members of the 33rd United States Colored Infantry are buried here.

Return to the cemetery and back into car. Get back on 21 and stay in the left lane, pull into the Wendy's' on your left. Walk over to the earthworks mounds on the left towards where you came from.

STOP 11:

FORT SAXTON

This fort was named after Brigadier General Rufus Saxton. It was constructed by the 1st New York Engineers and was armed with 3-inch siege howitzers, protecting Battery Creek and the Beaufort River.

Earthworks of Battery Saxton that protected the Beaufort River and Battery Creek.

The earthworks were built in 1862 by the 1st New York Engineers.

End Tour

Chapter 6

ST. HELENA ISLAND DRIVING TOUR

Take US 21 South and cross the bridge onto St. Helena Island and drive 6.4 miles to Martin Luther King Drive, turn right and continue 1.5 miles to the Penn Center.

STOP 1:

PENN CENTER,

16 PENN CENTER CIRCLE WEST

"Can you imagine anything more wonderful than a colored abolitionist meeting on a South Carolina plantation? There were collected all the free slaves on this island, listening to the most ultra abolition speeches that could be made, while two years ago their masters were still here. It's the most extraordinary change,"

Lieutenant Colonel Robert Gould Shaw
writing to his mother from St. Helena
Island in early July 1863.[62]

The Penn School was founded in 1862, when young abolitionist women from the large cities of the Northeast came to St. Helena to educate the African-American population. Today, it is a museum and educational center. The museum contains some artifacts from when the school first opened. The library has over two thousand photographs from the late nineteenth century. The Penn School was named a historic landmark in 1974.

The museum is open Monday – Saturday, 11:00 a.m. to 4:00 p.m.
(843) 838-2432
www.penncenter.com

A school was established here to provide education for the freed slaves. *Courtesy of the Library of Congress.*

Turn right onto Martin Luther King Drive and drive .1 miles and turn left into the church ruins on your left.

STOP 2:

CHAPEL OF EASE,

LANDS END ROAD

This was an active church before and during the war. It burned in 1886.

The Chapel of Ease burned in 1886.

Turn left onto Lands End Road, drive about 3 miles, and turn right onto Bay Point Road, follow road to beach.

STOP 3:

APPROXIMATE LOCATION OF

FORT BEAUREGARD

"Our fire was directed almost exclusively at the larger vessels. They were seen to be struck repeatedly, but the distance, never less than 2,500 yards, prevented our ascertaining the extent of injury."

**Captain Stephen Elliott, who
helped defend the fortification.**[63]

The fort was located on nearby St. Phillip's Island; it contained a battery that was designed to create enfilade fire to any vessels that steamed passed Fort Walker. This fort protected the Beaufort River and Beaufort, itself. The armament at the fort contained nineteen guns, including a 10-inch Columbiad.[64] The Beaufort Volunteer Artillery Company and the 12th South Carolina Infantry was stationed here during the Union attack on Port Royal on November 7, 1861.[65] The earthworks had thirteen guns and was renamed Fort Seward in 1862.

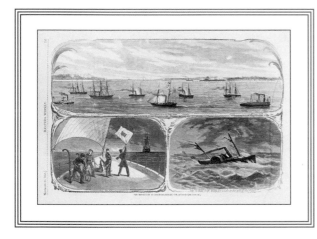

The Union navy gathers in Port Royal to assault forts Walker and Beauregard. *Courtesy of the Library of Congress.*

Fort Beauregard after the retreat of its Confederate defenders. *Courtesy of the Library of Congress.*

Confederate troops defending against the attack on November 7, 1861.

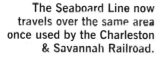
The Seaboard Line now travels over the same area once used by the Charleston & Savannah Railroad.

Turn back around towards Lands End Road, turn left, follow it until it intersects with US 21 North, turn left and drive back into historic Beaufort.

End Tour

Chapter 7

DRIVING TOUR OF THE FIGHTING AROUND THE CHARLESTON & SAVANNAH RAILROAD

From Beaufort, turn onto US 21 North towards Garden's Corner.

GARDEN'S CORNER

Charleston & Savannah Railroad

This railroad was completed in 1860. It was designed to move freight and passengers through this 110 mile stretch between the two cities. There were many stops along the way that would see much military action between 1862-65.

After the fall of Hilton Head, General Robert E. Lee spread his men along the railroad, which traversed along the marsh. The line crossed bridges over the Savannah, New, Tulliffinny, Pocotaligo, Salkehatchie, Combahee, and Coosawhatchie rivers, all of which were within range of General Thomas Sherman's troops based at Hilton Head and Beaufort.[66] This improvement in the defenses was done to keep any breach from occurring.

General Isaac Stevens, after the occupation of Beaufort, urged for action inland to cut the railroad line, so that Union troops could move either northward along the railroad towards Charleston or southward towards Savannah. He believed that the naval strength in the area was sufficient to support a strike against either city. Almost three weeks later, on December 31, 1861, he was allowed to foray inland, but was not permitted to go any further than Garden's Corner, the present day intersection of US routes 17 and 21. Lee had just fortified this section of the line, expecting such an attack.[67]

That morning, through a heavy mist, Stevens loaded his men on flats and other shallow-draft vessels, transporting them from Port Royal Island and Seabrook Landing. The following day they encountered Confederate units, who had been ordered to hold unless the attack was pressed. Naval artillery gave the Union force the advantage. The Confederate forces consisted of a contingent of Colonel James Jones' 14th South Carolina Infantry; they delayed the Unionists long enough to pull back the large caliber guns. Union gunboats proceeded to shell Gardner's Corner.[68] Stevens later withdrew his forces to Beaufort.

On March 2, 1862, Lee was ordered to Richmond as an advisor to Davis. His replacement was Pennsylvania born General John C. Pemberton. Pemberton would later be ordered to command the defenses at Vicksburg, Mississippi. By mid-April, Richmond had stripped the coastal defenses to reinforce the Confederate armies in Virginia and Tennessee, so he would have to defend the entire length of the railroad with limited troops. Pemberton moved the bulk of his remaining forces to Charleston, relying on cavalry patrols to keep the line open.[69] Stevens was never able to cut the line; he and his command were later ordered to join the newly formed Army of Virginia in July 1862. He fell at Second Manassas the next month.

Confederate cavalry units after April 1862 patrolled the length of the railroad.

Confederate artillery batteries were used to protect the bridges of the Charleston & Savannah Railroad. *Courtesy of the Library of Congress.*

The cavalry would try to thwart any Union attempt to cut the rail line. *Courtesy of the Library of Congress.*

Union dead from a raid against Garden's Corner in early January 1862.

Once reaching the intersection of US 17, turn left onto 17 South, make the next right onto Old Sheldon Church Road. Travel 1.7 miles and stop at the Church that will appear on your right.

STOP 1:

OLD SHELDON CHURCH RUINS

The original church was built between 1745 and 1755, burned by British troops in 1779. It was later rebuilt in 1826. It was burned by Union troops of General Oliver O. Howard's Corps on January 14, 1865, for it had been used by the Confederates as a hospital to treat small pox.

The walls remain today and it is a spectacular place to visit. It truly is stepping back into the antebellum period. This is a National Register of Historic Places site.

Old Sheldon Church was torched by Union troops in January 1865.

It was also burned by British troops in 1779.

Special religious services are still held here.

An interior view of the burned out church.

Turn around and head back to US 17 South, turn right and travel 7 miles to Pocotaligo. Turn left into the Visitor's Center.

POCOTALIGO

STOP 2:

LOW COUNTRY VISITOR CENTER

& MUSEUM,

FRAMPTON PLANTATION

The Confederate fortifications here were used as a fall back line, the Frampton Line, to help defend the Charleston & Savannah Railroad, which ran about a mile west of here. Much of the existing defenses were destroyed during the widening of US 17.

Union General Isaac Stevens' idea was to move up on the railroad. He had scouts behind Confederate lines that studied the Charleston and Savannah Railroad, observing the placement of bridges, trestles, strong points, and the movement of troops. Stevens led a foray into this area in February 1862, using the Combahee River as a guide to engage 4,000 Confederate troops along the rails between the Ashepoo and Savannah Rivers, near Pocotaligo. Stevens' plan was to throw a brigade against the railroad, destroy all the bridges south of the Ashepoo, about thirty miles worth of track. Then the plan was to counter march to Beaufort and attack Charleston by taking Church Flats fourteen miles south of Charleston, in the hope of stopping the flow of Southern reinforcements. His plan was rejected due to the imminent attack on Fort Pulaski, east of Savannah.[70]

He did get permission to stage a small raid at the head of the Broad River against the Confederate defenses at Pocotaligo. Union Colonel Benjamin Crist's force crossed the Coasaw River, coming ashore at the Port Royal Ferry on May 29. They moved past Gardens Corner, up the Sheldon Road, but much of his support was three hours behind.[71] Outside Gardens Corner, Confederate skirmishers stalled the Yankee column, forcing Crist to deploy a line of battle to break up the Confederate nuisance, but by then they had disappeared into the woods. These snipers continued to delay Crist's advance on Pocotaligo,. Confederate resistance stiffened as Union reinforcements arrived.[72]

The Union troops ran up against a well fortified position across a salt creek outside of town. Three hundred troops were able to force the Confederates to withdraw, but they held for the arrival of the 1st Connecticut Light Artillery.[73]

Confederate reinforcements arrived by train and Union troops were forced to withdraw due to lack of ammunition. They fell back to the Port Royal landing area. Confederate cavalry pursued, but were four hours late. The Federals safely returned to Beaufort.

On October 22, 1862, Mitchell ordered Brigadier General J. M. Brannan to take a force of 4,500 men to MacKay's Point and to take the Confederate Headquarters at Pocotaligo, trying to break the railroad line.[74] They were unable to break the Southern defenses. This house was burned by advancing Union troops in 1865 and was rebuilt in 1868

Open daily from 8:30 a.m. to 5:00 p.m.

The Frampton Line: these earthworks were created to protect the Charleston & Savannah Railroad, which ran about a mile west of this location.

The Frampton House was rebuilt in 1868, after being destroyed by Union forces in 1865.

Confederate troops defend the railroad at Pocotaligo on May 29, 1862.

Union troops were unable to dislodge the Southerners from Pocotaligo on May 29, 1862.

Union artillery was late in arriving, an opportunity missed on May 29.

Return to US 17 South, eventually it will merge with Interstate 95. You will only be on it for a few miles. As you drive south, you will pass through Coosawhatchie.

COOSAWATCHIE

"The enemy having complete possession of the waters and navigation (in and around Port Royal Sound, commands all the islands on the coast) and threatens both Savannah and Charleston and can come within four miles of this place. His sloops of war and large steamers can come up the Broad River to MacKay's Point, the mouth of the Pocotaligo and his gunboats can ascend some distance above the Coosawhatchie and Tulliffinny Rivers. We have no resources, but to prepare to meet them in the field,"

General Lee writing to Secretary of War
W. Judah Benjamin in late November 1861,
explaining the situation in the Low Country.[75]

This town is located at about midway on the Charleston & Savannah Railroad, so Lee established his headquarters here to have the ability to shuttle up and down the line to areas that were threatened. He arrived on November 7, 1861, on the orders of President Jefferson Davis. Upon his arrival, Hilton Head had fallen, so Lee asked Davis for reinforcements, additional artillery and infantry.[76] He received some, but not as much he would have liked.

After the Union failure at Honey Hill, a bid to cut the Charleston and Savannah Railroad in November 1864, their forces concentrated here. They had moved up the Broad River and landed at Gregory's Neck, marching as far as the Beaufort-Savannah Highway, present day SC 170. At this point, they skirmished with the Southern defenders, but were unable to reach the railroad.

The Federal gunboats *Pawnee* and *Sonoma* were deployed up the Coosawhatchie River on December 5, 1864, and destroyed a Confederate battery east of the town of Coosawhatchie. Foster had ordered this force to harass the Charleston & Savannah Railroad. The troops landed at the confluence of the Coosawhatchie and Tulifinny Rivers. On the 6th, they used the Tulifinny as a guide as they moved toward Coosawhatchie.[77]

Almost immediately they began to tangle with Confederate pickets between December 7 – 9th. The Confederates had tried to counter the Union thrust, but were repeatedly thrown back. This Union move was made to prevent reinforcements from reaching Savannah from Charleston. Hatch sent 500 men with axes, under the cover of skirmishers, and cut the trees to allow the deployment of artillery. Fighting took place between South Carolina Militia and United States' Marines.[78] Hatch was able to position his artillery so that they were trained to fire along the wide lane cut through the forest. The trains were now in direct and unobstructed range.

General Robert E. Lee established his department headquarters at Coosawhatchie in November 1861. *Courtesy of the Library of Congress.*

Continue driving south on US 17 and Interstate 95 towards Ridgeland. Exit onto SC 336 to the left; follow 336 into Ridgeland. You will be on 336 for about three miles when you pass through the Honey Hill Battlefield. You may stop anywhere near the Honey Hill housing development.

RIDGELAND

STOP 3:

HONEY HILL BATTLEFIELD

In late November 1864, Union Major General John G. Foster, commander of the Department of the South, ordered an expedition from Hilton Head to cut the Charleston and Savannah Railroad. It was undertaken in an effort to prevent the Confederates from rushing reinforcements by rail to oppose Sherman's advance towards Savannah. Major General John P. Hatch set out with 5,500 men on November 28, steaming up the Broad River in transports. Union intelligence was poor, so they became disoriented because of inadequate maps, and they became delayed. They disembarked at Boyd's Neck and marched inland toward Grahamville on November 30.

They met 2,000 Confederate defenders at Honey Hill, three miles from a depot on the railroad. Confederate Colonel Colcock, with a small number of cavalry and a 12-pound field piece, fought a delaying action. The South Carolina and Georgia infantry were under the command of General Gustavus W. Smith. Hatch approached Honey Hill over a narrow road with wetlands on both sides of the road; as they rounded the road they came under range of Confederate fire. They marched in a careless fashion, not using scouts or flankers as they probed the Confederate defenses. On one side of the road of their advance was a field full of tall broom with a marsh on the other side. The Confederates put a gun in the middle of the road, firing short-range ordinance until the road was cleared of the advancing troops. Colcock then set the broom ablaze forcing the Union troops back to Honey Hill.[79] Hatch made three frontal attacks, but each time was driven back by Confederate infantry and artillery. They were protected by a mile of earthworks, stretching from the Coosawhatchie to the Honey Hill Road.[80] Foster did not arrive until four hours after the battle began, but Hatch had already ordered a retreat back to Boyd's Landing. Union losses were 746 and the Confederate losses were 52.[81] This force would later try to disrupt the railroad near Coosawhatchie, between the Coosawhatchie and Tulifinny Rivers.

A view today of the Union advance at Honey Hill on November 30, 1864.

Union troops would be forced to retire after the surrounding brush was set afire.

A Union rear guard
action at Honey Hill.

A withdrawal was
ordered even though
they outnumbered the
Confederates almost
four to one.

A Federal battle line
near Honey Hill.

Strong Rebel resistance at Honey Hill kept Savannah safe for another month.

Turn back onto 336 and turn left onto the intersection of SC 462, heading back to Interstate 95. Tour over.

End Tour

Chapter 8

DAUFUSKIE ISLAND, THE SPRING BOARD AGAINST SAVANNAH TOUR

"There doesn't seem to be any doubt as to the result of the pending engagement—and if we are successful it is the opinion of a good many that the war can't last long....It is my opinion if we do not lick the Rebels in 6 months more the difficulty will be settled either by ourselves or the interventions of foreign powers. In either case we should probably return home—if the former—in peace, and if the latter, for home protection,"
Sergeant William Johnson, of the 7th Connecticut Infantry, was stationed on Daufuskie during the build up against Fort Pulaski in January 1862.[82]

To reach Daufuskie you will need to access a ferry to either Haig Point or Melrose. Rent a golf cart and obtain a map of the island; this will help you locate these sights. They are all marked on those maps.

Before the war there were eleven cotton plantations on the island; John Stoddard of Savannah owned six of these. The planters evacuated the island just before the Union landings on Hilton Head, November 7, 1861; the slaves were left in charge. The property was confiscated by Union troops and was designated as "abandoned lands." Taxes were soon levied against the properties.[83]

A Confederate raiding party from Bluffton landed on the island on January 30, 1863. They seized provisions, furniture, and slaves. Most of the furniture was sent to the people of Fredericksburg, Virginia, after the looting of the town by Burnside's Army of the Potomac in December 1862.[84]

Right:
Bloody Point, with Fort Pulaski in the distance.

BLOODY POINT

"A Machine was rigged for sawing of[f] the spiels close to the mud in fifteen feet of water we sawed of[f] twenty two in three nights and raised the hulk in three more the way is now clear for our Gun Boats."
**Sergeant William Johnson of the
7th Connecticut Infantry as they cleared
trees to build artillery fortifications on the
islands west of Fort Pulaski.**[85]

This is the southernmost part of Daufuskie Island and, on a clear day in early 1862, one could see in the distance the Confederate Stars and Bars flapping in the wind over Fort Pulaski, the protector of Savannah. This area, because of its proximity to Fort Pulaski, was used as a staging area for establishing Union gun batteries three miles up the Savannah River from Fort Pulaski. These batteries prevented the flow of supplies and reinforcements from Savannah to the fort. Daufuskie was used as a base to cut off communications with Fort Pulaski; gun batteries were placed on Tybee, Jones, Long, and Bird Islands. These were all along the Savannah River, forcing the stoppage of supplies from Savannah to the fort.[86]

Engineers from Daufuskie cleared the obstructions placed by the Confederates at Wall's Cut, allowing Union gunboats to patrol that area of the Savannah River. Later trees were cut down here to build a corduroy road across Jones Island to establish a battery at Venus Point. Work was done at night in order to avoid detection.[87]

The Dunn Mansion was located on high ground in Bloody Point; from there Union soldiers could hear and see the bombardment of Fort Pulaski in April 1862.[88]

Union troops cut down trees to help build artillery batteries three miles west of Fort Pulaski on the Savannah River.

Fort Pulaski, the target of Union troops on Daufuskie in April 1862.

BLOODY POINT LIGHTHOUSE

John Michael Doyle, the first Bloody Point lighthouse keeper, enlisted in the 82nd Ohio Infantry in December 1861. Doyle saw action in the first year and a half of the war in the Shenandoah Valley. After participating in the Battle of Second Manassas, his regiment was assigned to the Army of the Potomac, serving from Antietam to Gettysburg. His corps was sent to Tennessee in October 1863 to help lift the siege of Chattanooga.

In April 1864, Doyle fought with Sherman in the Atlanta Campaign and marched with Sherman to Savannah and through the Carolinas.

After the war, Doyle helped build lighthouses in the early 1880s. He helped construct the lighthouses on Parris Island and Bloody Point. He was appointed keeper of the Bloody Point Lighthouse on April 4, 1883, and served this post until he resigned on August 15, 1890.[89] He is buried in Savannah's Catholic Cemetery.

Robert Augustus Sisson was the second lighthouse keeper here. He assumed the position on August 15, 1890, from John Michael Doyle. His regiment, the 157th New York, was brigaded with Doyle's regiment while in service with the Army of the Potomac.[90] Sisson's first action was at the Battle of Chancellorsville. As part of the 11th Corps, they were hit hard under Jackson's flank attack. They were later mauled on the first and third days at Gettysburg. That fall, Sisson and his regiment were transferred to the South Carolina Low Country; his unit was assigned to the Department of the South. Initially, he saw siege duty at Charleston. In late 1864, he fought at Honey Hill and was mustered out near Charleston in the summer of 1865. Sisson went to work after the war with the United States' Lighthouse Service and would serve at Bloody Point until relieved by his son in May 1908.

HAIG POINT

"I could sell three thousand Cigars and three or four Gross of Chewing Tobacco in two days for cash and make from 40 to 50 dollars on it.... I am glad that the watches are a coming as I think I can dispose of them to good advantage."

Sergeant Johnson, he earned extra money by speculating on watches, chewing tobacco, cigars, and other goods forwarded to him by family and friends from the North.[91]

This plantation was owned by Squire Pope, who had numerous cotton plantations on Hilton Head Island and a summer home along the May River in Bluffton. The war took its toll on Pope, who lost many relatives early in the war. He died at Sandersville, Georgia, in March 1862.[92]

Union Brigadier General Ebert L. Viele was stationed on the island in January 1862. Viele's brigade consisted of infantry from the 8th Maine, 28th Massachusetts, 3rd New Hampshire, 6th and 7th Connecticut, the 46th, 47th, and 48th New York, and the 3rd Rhode Island Artillery. These troops disembarked at Haig's Point, while the engineers built a wharf on the New River. During the occupation these troops were placed at the Cooper River Landing and the Dunn Plantation on Mungin Creek. The mansion was used as quarters for the officers.[93]

Washington called on General Hunter to send these troops to join McClellan's army in July 1862, so he ordered the evacuation of the island on July 3.[94]

Ruins of slave quarters at Haig Point.

Tabby ruins of a slave's quarters.

A woman reenacts slave life on a Low Country Plantation.

Union troops just after disembarking on Daufuskie.

MELROSE

"The sergeant major and myself started on a ramp and walked down the island a mile and turned to the shore and followed the beach down for two miles to a plantation called the Stoddard Place, a finer never was, large elegant and tasteful mansion with an abundance of outbuildings,"
Lieutenant Charles F. Monroe of the 8th Maine Infantry remarking on the beauty of the mansion at Melrose.[95]

The house was owned by John Stoddard, who lived in Savannah. He sold cotton to the Savannah market. In 1857, he freed most of his slaves.

The mansion, in early 1862, housed female missionaries from the Northeast who taught eighty-six African-American children from the Melrose School for the Free.

The mansion burned in 1912.

Former building used by slaves, built sometime in the 1850s.

Aerial view of Bloody Point Beach, where Union troops relaxed.

End Tour

Chapter 9
MAPS

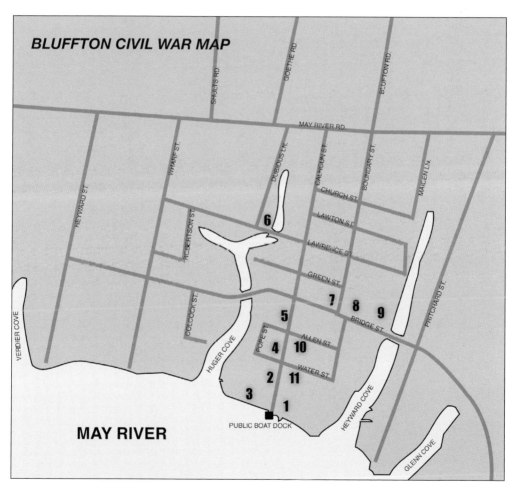

Map of Bluffton Walking Tour.

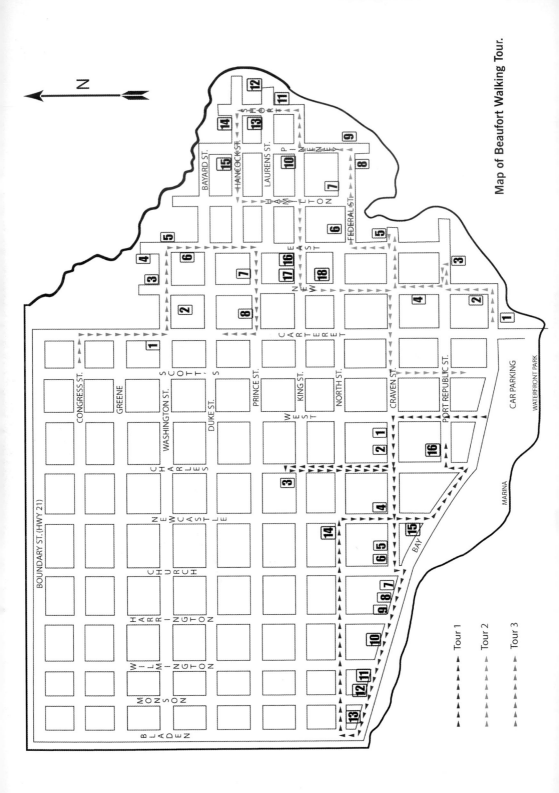

Map of Beaufort Walking Tour.

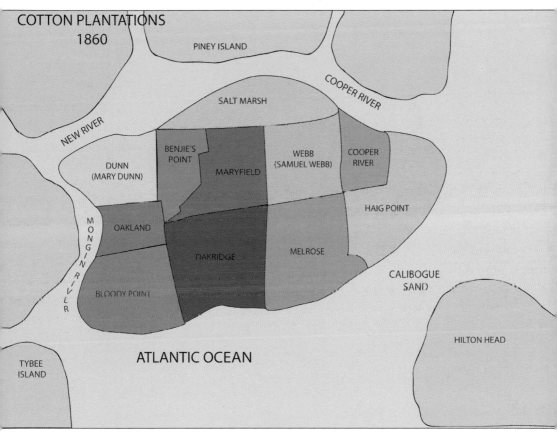

COTTON PLANTATIONS
1860

PINEY ISLAND

COOPER RIVER

SALT MARSH

NEW RIVER

BENJIE'S
POINT

WEBB
(SAMUEL WEBB)

COOPER
RIVER

DUNN
(MARY DUNN)

MARYFIELD

HAIG POINT

MONGIN RIVER

OAKLAND

OAKRIDGE

MELROSE

CALIBOGUE
SAND

BLOODY POINT

HILTON HEAD

TYBEE
ISLAND

ATLANTIC OCEAN

Map of Daufuskie Cotton Plantations in 1860.

BIBLIOGRAPHY

Burchard, Peter. *One Gallant Rush.* New York: St. Martin's Press, 1965.

Burn, Billie. *An Island Named Daufuskie*. Spartanburg, South Carolina: Reprint Company, 1991.

Carse, Robert. *Hilton Head Island in the Civil War*. Columbia, South Carolina: The State Printing Company, 1981.

Charleston Mercury, 6 June 1863.

Chestnut, Mary. *Mary Chestnut's Civil War*. Ed. C. Vann Woodward. New Haven & London: Yale University Press, 1981.

Conner, T. D. *Homemade Thunder: War on the South Coast 1861-1865*. Savannah, Georgia: Writeplace Press, 2004.

Coombe, Jack D. *Gunsmoke over the Atlantic*. New York: Bantam Books, 2002.

D'Arcy, David & Ben Mammina. *Civil War Walking Tour of Savannah*. Atglen, Pennsylvania: Schiffer Publishing, 2006.

Donnelly, Ralph W. *The Confederate States' Marine Corps: The Rebel Leathernecks*. Shippensberg, Pennsylvania: White Mane Publishing Company, 1981.

Graydon, Nell. *Tales of Beaufort.* Beaufort, South Carolina: Beaufort Books Shop Inc., 1963.

Holmgren, Virginia C. *Hilton Head: A Sea Island Chronicle*. Hilton Head Island, South Carolina: Hilton Head Island Publishing Company, 1959.

Kennedy, Frances H. *The Civil War Battlefield Guide*. New York & Boston: Houghton Mifflin, 1998.

Peeples, Robert E. H. *Tales of Antebellum Hilton Head Families: Hilton Head and Our Family Circle*. 1970.

Rhea, Gordon C. *The Battles For Spotsylvania Court House and the Road to Yellow Tavern, May 7-12, 1864*. Baton Rouge & London: Louisiana State Press, 1997.

Stevenson, Peter & Evelene. *The Spirit of Old Beaufort*. Beaufort, South Carolina: The Spirit of Old Beaufort, 2000.

Time-Life Books Editors. *Charleston: Voices of the Civil War*. Alexandria, Virginia: Time-Life Books, 1997.

van Doren Stern, Philip. *The Confederate Navy: A Pictorial History.* New York: Da Capo Press, 1992.

Weiner, Marli F., ed. *A Heritage of Woe: The Civil War Diary of Grace Brown Elmore 1861-1868.* Athens & London: University of Georgia Press, 1997.

ENDNOTES

1. Connor, T. D. *Homemade Thunder: War on the South Coast 1861-1865* (Savannah, GA: Writeplace Press, 2004), 45.

2. Peeples, Robert E. H. *Tales of Antebellum Hilton Head Families: Hilton Head and Our Family Circle* (1970), 14.

3. Holmgren, Virginia C. *Hilton Head: A Sea Island Chronicle* (Hilton Head Island, SC: Hilton Head Island Publishing Company 1959), 66.

4. Graydon, Nell. *Tales of Beaufort* (Beaufort, SC: Beaufort Books Shop Inc, 1963), 96.

5. Mary Chestnut's Civil War, edited by C. Vann Woodward (Yale University Press New Haven & London, 1981), 232

6. Beaufort County, 22.

7. Holmgren, 95.

8. *Charleston Mercury* 6 June 1863.

9. Beaufort County, 23

10. *Charleston Mercury* 6 June 1863.

11. Beaufort County, South Carolina (Beaufort, SC: Beaufort County Chamber of Commerce, 1953), 23

12. *Charleston Mercury* 6 June 1863.

13. Peeples, 12.

14. Holmgren, 80.

15. *Ibid*, 81

16. *Ibid.*

17. Connor, 55.

18. Connor, 49.

19. Donnelly, Ralph W. *The Confederate States Marine Corps: The Rebel Leathernecks* (Shippensberg, PA: White Mane Publishing Company, 1981), 90.

20. Connor, 51.

21. Peeples, 13.

22. Donnelly, 90.

23. www.answers.com/topic/Mitchellville

24. Connor, 103.

25. Peeples, 14.

26. Coombe, Jack D. *Gunsmoke over the Atlantic* (New York: Bantam Books, 2002), 61.

27. Carse, Robert. *Hilton Head Island in the Civil War* (Columbia, SC: The State Printing Company, 1981), 82.

28. Holmgren, 84.

29. www.westvillenj.com/westvilleand thecivilwar

30. Connor, 101.

31. *Ibid*, 96.

32. www.civilweek.com/1862/oct1862.htm

33. van Doren Stern, Philip. *The Confederate Navy: A Pictorial History* (New York: Da Capo Press, 1992), 138.

34. Graydon, 107.

35. Holmgren, 95.

36. Connor, 101.

37. *Ibid*, 102.

38. *Ibid*, 61.

39. Stevenson, Peter & Evelene. *The Spirit of Old Beaufort* (Beaufort, SC: The Spirit of Old Beaufort, 2000), 6.

40. *Ibid,* 7.

41. *Ibid,* 15.

42. Graydon, 88.

43. Stevenson, 14.

44. *Ibid*, 13.

45. *Ibid*, 11.

46. *Ibid*.

47. *Ibid*, 21.

48. Graydon, 9.

49. *Ibid*, 9.

50. *Ibid*.

51. http://www.chicora.org/heritage_not_hate.htm

52. Editors of Time-Life Books. *Charleston, Voices of the Civil War* (Alexandria, VA· Time-Life Books 1997), 136.

53. *Ibid*, 23.

54. *Ibid,* 21.

55. *Ibid,* 25.

56. *Ibid*, 28.

57. Rhea, Gordon C. *The Battles For Spotsylvania Court House and the Road to Yellow Tavern, May 7-12, 1864* (Baton Rouge & London: Louisiana State Press, 1997), 28.

58. www.beauforttours.com/beaufortarsenal/index.htm

59. Connor, 87.

60. *Ibid*, 89.

61. *Ibid*, 91.

62. Burchard, Peter. *One Gallant Rush* (New York: St. Martin's Press, 1965), 117.

63. http://civilwargazette.wordpress.com/2007/01/04/the-capture-of-port-royal-november-1861-cmh/

64. Coombe, 59.

65. Connor, 55.

66. *Ibid,* 61.

67. *Ibid,* 62.

68. *Ibid,* 63.

69. *Ibid,* 64.

70. *Ibid,* 92.

71. *Ibid.*

72. *Ibid,* 93.

73. *Ibid.*

74. *Ibid,*108.

75. *Ibid,* 60.

76. *Ibid,* 59.

77. Carse, 142.

78. *Ibid.*

79. *Ibid*, 140.

80. *Ibid*, 141.

81. Kennedy, Frances H. *The Civil War Battlefield Guide* (New York & Boston: Houghton Mifflin: 1998), 100.

82. http://www.sc.edu/library/socar/uscs/1995/whjohn95.html

83. Burn, Billie. *An Island Named Daufuskie* (Spartanburg, SC: Reprint Company, 1991), 135.

84. *Ibid.*

85. http://www.sc.edu/library/socar/uscs/1995/whjohn95.html

86. *Ibid.*

87. Burn, 242.

88. *Ibid,* 240.

89. *Ibid,* 207.

90. *Ibid*, 209.

91. http://www.sc.edu/library/socar/uscs/1995/whjohn95.html

92. Burn, 241.

93. *Ibid*, 240.

94. Connor, 101.

95. Burn, 109.